AF228532

BABY COWS

Cody Koala

An Imprint of Pop!
popbooksonline.com

abdobooks.com

Published by Pop!, a division of ABDO, PO Box 398166, Minneapolis, Minnesota 55439. Copyright © 2021 by POP, LLC. International copyrights reserved in all countries. No part of this book may be reproduced in any form without written permission from the publisher. Pop!™ is a trademark and logo of POP, LLC.

Printed in the United States of America, North Mankato, Minnesota

052020
092020

THIS BOOK CONTAINS RECYCLED MATERIALS

Cover Photo: Shutterstock Images

Interior Photos: Shutterstock Images, 1, 15 (top), 15 (bottom left), 15 (bottom right), 19, 20; iStockphoto, 5 (top), 5 (bottom left), 5 (bottom right), 6, 8–9, 11, 12, 16

Editor: Nick Rebman
Series Designer: Christine Ha

Library of Congress Control Number: 2019954949

Publisher's Cataloging-in-Publication Data

Names: London, Martha, author.
Title: Baby cows / by Martha London
Description: Minneapolis, Minnesota : POP!, 2021 | Series: Baby farm animals | Includes online resources and index
Identifiers: ISBN 9781532167430 (lib. bdg.) | ISBN 9781532168536 (ebook)
Subjects: LCSH: Cattle--Infancy--Juvenile literature. | Calves--Juvenile literature. | Baby farm animals--Juvenile literature. | Animal babies--Juvenile literature.
Classification: DDC 636.2--dc23

Hello! My name is

Cody Koala

Pop open this book and you'll find QR codes like this one, loaded with information, so you can learn even more!

Scan this code* and others like it while you read, or visit the website below to make this book pop.

popbooksonline.com/baby-cows

*Scanning QR codes requires a web-enabled smart device with a QR code reader app and a camera.

Table of Contents

Chapter 1

On the Farm

Baby cows are called calves. Female calves are known as heifers. Male calves are known as bulls. Calves are **mammals**. They drink milk from their mothers.

Watch a video here!

Calves stay close to their mothers. Cows live in groups called **herds**. Some farms have cows for milk. Other farms have cows for meat.

Chapter 2

Soft and Fluffy

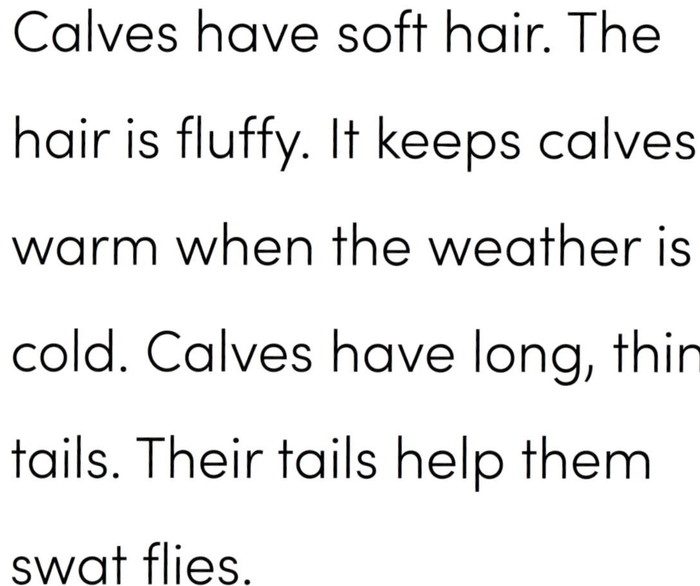

Calves have soft hair. The hair is fluffy. It keeps calves warm when the weather is cold. Calves have long, thin tails. Their tails help them swat flies.

Learn more here!

Calves have big ears. They listen for their mothers' calls. They follow their mothers across the fields.

eye
ear
leg
hoof

Calves have hard **hooves**.
Hooves help calves walk on
rocks. Calves run and play.
Then they sleep in the grass.

Chapter 3

Growing Up

Calves drink milk when they are young. But soon calves begin to eat grass. They wander away from their mothers and explore the fields.

Learn more here!

Calves gain weight quickly. Soon they are big enough to be **weaned**. Farmers separate the calves from their mothers. The calves live together. They play together in a field away from the other cows.

Chapter 4

Part of the Herd

Sometimes farmers sell calves after they are **weaned**. Most farms are businesses. Farmers make money when they sell calves.

Complete an
activity here!

Dairy heifers stay on the farm. A heifer becomes an adult after it gives birth to its first calf. Dairy cows produce milk. Farmers sell the milk.

Making Connections

Text-to-Self

Imagine you are on a farm. What would it be like to see a baby cow?

Text-to-Text

What other books about baby animals have you read? How are calves similar to and different from those animals?

Text-to-World

Why do you think calves are important for farms?

Glossary

dairy – having to do with milk, or foods made from milk, including cheese, yogurt, and butter.

herd – a large group of animals that live and travel together.

hooves – the hard parts that cover an animal's feet.

mammal – a type of animal that has hair or fur and feeds milk to its young.

wean – to teach an animal to eat food that is not its mother's milk.

Index

Online Resources

popbooksonline.com

Thanks for reading this Cody Koala book!

Scan this code* and others like it in this book, or visit the website below to make this book pop!

popbooksonline.com/baby-cows

*Scanning QR codes requires a web-enabled smart device with a QR code reader app and a camera.